The

Manufacturer's
MANUAL

Discovering the Purpose of You, the Product

By ALLEN S. WILSON

Lightning Fast Book Publishing, LLC
P.O. Box 441328
Fort Washington, MD 20744

www.lfbookpublishing.com

All rights reserved. No part of this book may be reproduced or transmitted in any form or by any means—electronic, mechanical, photocopying, recording, or otherwise—without written permission from the author, except for the inclusion of brief quotations in a review.

The author of this book shares strategies for understanding your capabilities and life purpose. The literary offering provided is non-fictional and derived from the experience and understanding of the author. The intent is to give readers a blueprint to self-awareness. In the event that you use or enact any of the material in this book, the author and publisher assume no responsibility for your actions.

The publisher, Lightning Fast Book Publishing, assumes no responsibility for any content presented in this book.

Copyright © 2018
Allen S. Wilson.
All rights reserved.

ISBN-10: 0-9994653-2-5
ISBN-13: 978-0-9994653-2-5

Appreciation:

To the Creator of all things with awe, humility, honor, and reverence who called me out of darkness into His marvelous light.

To my wife, Marsha. A king has a crown. The crown of a king is his wife. Thank you for being my crown as I grow into the king I was sent to be before the foundations of the world were laid. He is King of kings and Lord of lords.

To my mother, Willie D. Wilson. I am grateful to the Father for you. Thank you for raising me to early adulthood during difficult times and challenges.

To Stanley D. Williams and Bethtina Q. Williams. Thank you for being father and mother, mentoring and coaching me into the mysteries of the Kingdom of God.

In memory of George D. Lee, III. Thank you for being a spiritual covering as a grandfather in the Kingdom of God.

To James D. Smith. I am thankful to the Father for you demonstrating an exemplary attitude of servanthood for the Father and to humanity.

To His Royal Majesty King Adamtey I (aka Dr. Kingsley A. Fletcher). I am greatly appreciative to the Father for your example of a king and priest to myself (and many others) as we move more into the demonstration of the Kingdom of God.

To Terrence V. Wilson. I am thankful to the Father for you recognizing gifts, talents, and abilities within me and giving me the opportunity to expand those gifts, talents, and abilities through serving others.

To Melvin Lawton, Stafford Tiny Patterson, and Clayton Goodwin. I am thankful to the Father and to you for our time in serving and growing together, discovering our purpose and increasing our potential while in Asia.

To Newlin B. Carter. I am greatly appreciative to the Father for you being an example to me in those early years of maturing.

To Joseph Belson, Anthony Simmons, and Darryl Wilson. I am greatly appreciative to the Father for you being my friends in those early years of maturing.

Table of Content

Preface 7

Message from the King (Creator) 9

Manufacturer 11

Chapter 1 Manual 13

Chapter 2 Purpose of the Product 19

Chapter 3 Meditation 23

Chapter 4 Method (First Thing First) 27

Chapter 5 The Game of Life 35

Chapter 6 Man 43

Chapter 7 Marriage (Covenant) 49

Chapter 8 Maintaining the Product 57

Chapter 9 Meals 63

Chapter 10 Medicine 69

Chapter 11 Money 79

Chapter 12 Making of a Disciple (Missing Link to Maturity) 85

Chapter 13 Ministry (Office) 91

Chapter 14 Music 97

Chapter 15 Media 103

Chapter 16 Message to the Nations from the Manufacturer 107

About the Author 113

References 115

Appendix 117

Preface

When we purchase a product such as a television, DVD player, or computer, we bring it home and open the box. Most of the time, a set of instructions or manual comes with the product. The set of instructions or manual is placed in such a way that when we open the box, we can reach for them easily or placed near the top of the box so we see it first. The manufacturer of the product wants all those using the product to see the set of instructions or manual before attempting to use or operate.

Warning – "Don't attempt to use or operate this product without reading the manual!"

or

"Attempting to use or operate this product without reading the manual may cause hazardous conditions!"

Most of us don't observe the warning(s). We open the box, remove the product, and start trying to operate the product without reading the manual. This opens the door to experimentation (trial and error) without guidance, direction, and/or controls (or boundaries) causing malfunction (failure and break down) and abuse (misuse and misapplication).

Message from the King (Creator) - Manufacturer

Warning – "Read the manual before attempting to use or operate the product."

Warning - "Attempting to use or operate the product without reading the manual may cause hazardous conditions."

The manufacturer created the product to serve a function. The function of a product was created to serve a need or solve a problem.

Warning – "Don't ask another (like or similar) product its purpose." "Ask the manufacturer."

"Don't ask another (like or similar) product how to operate." "Go to the Manufacturer's Manual."

"Experimenting with the product (male and female respectively) without reading the Manufacturer's Manual is not recommended."

History is really the unfolding of the product's (mankind) attempt to operate and experiment independently of the manufacturer. Read the Manufacturer's Manual so not to create Jesus Christ in your (or our) own image. Instead, see and discover Jesus Christ as the representation of the manufacturer (or creator) and a model to emulate.

Manufacturer

What was in the mind of the manufacturer before He created mankind? Why did the manufacturer create you? What did the manufacturer want you to accomplish before sending you from the unseen realm to the seen realm? Before the manufacturer creates a product, He must determine the purpose which the product will fulfill. The purpose the product is created for remains the reason why the product came into existence. The purpose for which the manufacturer created the product (mankind) was to reveal to all creation (both seen and unseen) the manifold wisdom of the manufacturer (or the creator). The manufacturer is the Father who created a family of children in the seen realm.

We can't change or alter the design of the product without the manufacturer's approval or permission. If we change or alter the product without the manufacturer's approval or permission, sooner or later, the product will not be used to its full potential or will stop operating.

Instructions to Benefit the Reader

> At the end of each chapter, there is a section for "Notes and Insights" to record as you read, meditate and discuss with others.

Chapter 1
Manual

The Manufacturer's Manual

A manual is a user guide and/or set of instructions to properly operate a product or to assemble or disassemble a product. A manual directs us on how to operate the product to fulfill the purpose or intent of the product. The manual is the only source of information or instructions for assembly, disassembly, and/or operation. Why would a product go to another source for information or instructions on assembly, disassembly, and/or operation?

The purpose of the manufacturer's manual is to transform the product (mankind) from a slavery mentality to a kingdom (fruitful, multiplying, overcoming, subduing, ruling, responsible, accountable) mentality. A slave has no sense of ownership, possession, or proprietorship. A slave has no sense self-worth. A slave has no sense of self-estimation (low self-esteem). A slave has no vision. A slave has no hope. A slave hate work because he or she identify work with pain or punishment. A slave has no esteem for himself or herself because he or she has taken on the mentality of his or her master. A slave hates his brother because of low self-esteem and his brother remind him of himself. A slave has a death wish. A slave wants to leave earth. A slave is afraid to live. A slave wants to die. Slavery and the results, consequences, or outcomes are really the unfolding of the product's attempts to operate and experiment independently of the manufacturer. Sometimes, the product will malfunction even if the product has started out with good intentions.

The purpose of the manufacturer's manual is to restore the slave (product) to the governing influence (rule, order, and structure), authority, principles, laws, culture, values, and lifestyle of the manufacturer to the product (humanity) because the product is malfunctioning, not working properly, and/or out of order. The manufacturer's manual instructs humanity to seek first the Kingdom

Discovering the Purpose of You, the Product

of God and His righteousness, and what is needed for humanity to operate properly will be added.

Warning – "Don't seek first education, social status, politics, fame, and/or money."

Contrary to contemporary (or modern) beliefs, the product's craving to first pursue water, food, shelter, transportation, protection, security, preservation, and significance through education, social status, politics, fame, and/or money independent of the manufacturer misleads the product and those associated or connected to the product. The manufacturer's manual gives us information on the nature of the manufacturer (creator), the origin of the product (mankind), the nature of the product, the purpose of the product, and the expectation(s) of the product. Seek to pursue, study, search, explore, discover, understand, learn, and preoccupy oneself with the manufacturer's manual to make better use of the product. Give priority above everything to seeking the manufacturer (creator of the product), the origin of the product (mankind), the nature of the product, the purpose of the product, and the expectation(s) of the product in the manufacturer's manual.

The manufacturer's manual is a legal book that allows someone to stand in right positioning or alignment with the manufacturer's authority, principles, laws, culture, values, and lifestyle leading to proper use of the product (male and female respectively), relationships, marriage, intercourse (sex), health, food, water, clothing, shelter, security, and transportation. The results of the manufacturer's communication with the product and the product's communication back to the manufacturer will be evident during the product's operations. In addition, the results of communication between the manufacturer and the product will show or demonstrate that the product is operating correctly or not. If

The Manufacturer's Manual

the product is not operating correctly, the product has an opportunity to read (pursue, study, search, or explore) the manufacturer's manual and communicate with the manufacturer throughout the product's existence.

Discovering the Purpose of You, the Product

Notes and Insights

The Manufacturer's Manual

Chapter 2
Purpose of the Product

The Manufacturer's Manual

The purpose for which the product is created remains the reason why the product came into existence. If you don't know why the product is, you will not understand the use of the product. The purpose determines the design of a product. A product is the way it is because of why it is. A product is the way it is because of why it was created. A product is created to meet a need, service, or function. God is the creator of all things. The creator created all things (or products) with a purpose. God created all things to fulfill a purpose in a form of a need, service, or function. The purpose determines the design of the product to fulfill the need, service, or function to be carried out.

Every product is the way it is because of why it was created. A product is the way it is because of what it is to accomplish. God designed everything to accomplish its purpose. The purpose of the product was in the mind of the manufacturer (or creator) before the product came into existence physically. Therefore, the purpose of a product determines the nature a product. The purpose of a product determines the design of the product. The purpose of a product determines the features (or components) of a product. The purpose of a product is determined by the need. The purpose for which the manufacturer created the product (mankind) was to reveal to all creation (both seen and unseen) the manifold wisdom of the manufacturer (or the creator).

Discovering the Purpose of You, the Product

Notes and Insights

The Manufacturer's Manual

Chapter 3

Meditation

The Manufacturer's Manual

Meditation means "to murmur" and has similar meanings to other words like mutter, whisper, mumble, and worry (or anxiety, fret, and fear). Whatever we meditate upon in our heart usually runs parallel with the words of our mouth. We need to learn how to change our meditation to line up with the manufacturer's instructions in His manual. Whatever the heart meditates upon is what the mouth will speak. As we learn to meditate upon the manufacturer's instructions in His manual, we will have fewer problems in understanding the nature of the manufacturer (or creator), the origin of the product (mankind), and the nature of the product.

We are designed by the manufacturer to speak whatever our hearts meditate upon, including our passions, emotions, and moods. Whatever we meditate upon will come out of the mouth. As we meditate upon manufacturer's instructions, the words of our mouth will become aligned with the meditation of our heart producing a result. Another word for meditation could be "worry," which is a form of meditation upon negative (or wrong) things or problem(s) day and night. We need to change our meditation to the remedy for our problems, yielding the right (or better) results in our attitudes, actions, and/or environment(s).

The remedy is the manufacturer's instructions to the product (or all humanity). "My word is health to all their flesh" (Book of Proverbs, chapter 4:20-27). His word is like medicine to all our flesh (or whole being). The Manufacturer's Manual will not depart out of my heart, but I will meditate (ponder, think) on the instructions written therein day and night, so to observe and do all that is written. Then, I will make my way prosperous and have good success operating the product. My mouth will speak in wisdom, and the meditation of my heart will be understanding.

Discovering the Purpose of You, the Product

Cud is an amount of food (semi-degraded) that returns from a ruminant's stomach to the mouth to be chewed for additional time (Cooper, Calottta (2012), The Complete Beginner's Guide to Raising Small Animals, pg 203). It is a Bolus (ball-like mixture) of food and saliva regurgitated from the reticulorumen (storage chamber) and forms in the mouth during the process of chewing for plant-eating mammals. Cud is produced during the physical digestive process of rumination. Ruminants are mammals that can acquire nutrients from plant-based food by fermenting it in a specialized stomach (storage chamber) prior to digestion through microbial activities. This process called foregut fermentation takes place in the front part of the digestion system and usually requires the fermented ingesta (known as cud) to be regurgitated and chewed again. The process of rechewing the cud to break down plant matter further and stimulate digestion is called rumination. The word "ruminant" comes from the Latin ruminare, meaning "to chew over again." Ruminant animals such as cattle, goats, sheep, and llamas "chew the cud" to process food for additional digestion. The expressions "chewing the cud" or "chewing one's cud" means meditating or pondering, and similar terminologies such as "he chewed that over for a bit" or "chew on that" have a similar origin.

Warning – "To maximize clarity and understanding of the manufacturer's manual, one must meditate (chew over again) or ponder on the information daily."

Prayer is an expression of thoughts that are on the inside of us. Meditation is the foundation of prayer because the mouth will only speak that which your heart is meditating upon. Meditation opens the door to two-way communication between the product (mankind) and the manufacturer (creator). Music can play an important part in meditation, which will be mentioned later.

The Manufacturer's Manual

Notes and Insights

Chapter 4

Method (First Thing First) - Questions

The Manufacturer's Manual

What happens when the product does not give priority above everything to seeking the manufacturer (creator of the product), the origin of the product (mankind), the nature of the product, the purpose of the product, and the expectation(s) of the product in the manufacturer's manual? What happens when the product tries to operate or solve problems independent of the manufacture's manual? What happens when the product asks another similar product how to operate instead of going to the manufacture and the manufacture's manual? What happens when the product uses the wrong method to approaching situations, challenges, or difficulties in life? What happens when the product uses an alternate method of instructions or operations? What happens when the product experiments (using trial and error) with itself or with other like products instead of following the manufacturer's manual?

What happens when the product does not give priority above everything to seeking the manufacturer (creator of the product), the origin of the product (mankind), the nature of the product, the purpose of the product, and the expectation(s) of the product in the manufacturer's manual? Priority above all others, highest valve, or above everything indicate there are other priorities that preoccupy our time, energy, creativity, and resources, not allowing us (the product) to focus on important endeavors or activities. The manufacturer's manual indicates or directs the product to seek first the manufacturer and right positioning or alignment. If the product is not in right positioning or alignment with the manufacturer, then abuse is inevitable, unavoidable, predictable, and/or foreseeable. For example, if the male (product) of humanity is not in alignment with the manufacturer (creator of the humanity), then the female (product) will be out of alignment causing the offspring (or descendants) to be out of alignment also. This includes matters concerning manhood, relationships, marriage,

Discovering the Purpose of You, the Product

intercourse (sex), health, consumption of food & water, leadership, education, money, peace, and security. In addition, laws, policies, and regulations produced by humanity will not be able to make up for the misalignment of humanity.

What happens when the product tries to operate or solve problems independent of the manufacturer's manual? When the product tries to operate or solve problems independent of the manufacturer's manual, there is no communication (or very little communication) between the manufacturer and the product. Malfunction can occur, abuse is unavoidable, and/or potential is wasted or lost.

What happens when the product asks another similar product how to operate instead of going to the manufacturer and the manufacturer's manual? How many times have we asked those around us their opinion on an issue or subject, including friends, educators, and/or medical professionals? How many times in our search for answers to many of life's situations or challenges have we looked to a variety of human governmental systems, including feudalism, imperialism, colonialism, humanism, communism, socialism, deism, communal living, dictatorship, and democracy? Living in a multitude of places throughout the world (including the United States, England, Korea, Germany, and Iraq) has given me an opportunity to be exposed to many forms of human governments (CIA World Factbook - The best country factbook, Retrieved from http://www.ciaworldfactbook.us/index.html). The product tends to seek or look to human governmental systems (Keenan, Edward, 1973, The Art of the Possible, An Everyday Guide to Politics):

- Feudalism - Combination of legal and military customs in medieval Europe that thrived between the 9th and 15th centuries. In addition, it was a means of structuring society

The Manufacturer's Manual

around relationships derived from the holding of land in exchange for service or labor.

- Imperialism - An accomplishment that includes a country (typically an empire or a kingdom) extending its power by the acquisition, procurement, or attainment of territories and resources. In addition, may include the exploitation of these territories, exploitation of the people within these territories, and associated with colonialism.

- Colonialism - An expression of imperialism.

- Humanism - A philosophical and ethical stance that stresses the worth and intervention of human beings individually and collectively.

- Communism - A system in which goods are owned in common and are available to all as needed promoting the elimination of private property or ownership.

- Oligarchy – A system of government in which powers and authority is in the hands of very few people.

- Socialism - A system or condition of society in which the means of production are owned and controlled by the state promoting no private property or ownership.

- Capitalism - An economic system and philosophy constructed on private ownership and investment as the means distribution of currency and exchange of currency for profit.

Discovering the Purpose of You, the Product

- Deism - The belief in the presence of a god on the evidence of reason and nature only with denial of supernatural revelation.

- Communal Living - meaning an intentional community of people or a large gathering of people sharing a common life, living together, sharing common interests, often having common values and beliefs with shared property, possessions, resources, work, income, and/or assets.

- Dictatorship - Dictatorship is an arrangement of government in which a country or a group of countries is governed by one person (a dictator) or by a polity (group). A dictatorship is a form of authoritarianism in which the dictator or an institution controls nearly every aspect of the public and private behavior of citizens. Also known as Autocracy.

- Absolute Monarchy - A form of government in which a person or monarch holds absolute power and authority over a country.

- Constitutional Monarchy - A form of government in which decisions are made by democratically elected legislature while the monarch serves as a symbolic leader and acts as a check to ensure that all laws are constitutional.

- Authoritarianism - A form of government characterized by strong central power and restricted political parties or groups. Individual freedoms are subordinate to the state and there is no constitutional accountability in an authoritarian government or country. Also known as fascism or totalitarianism.

The Manufacturer's Manual

- Democracy ("rule of the people" or "rule of the majority") - A system of government in which the citizens' exercise power directly or elect representatives from among themselves to form a governing body.

Democracy may be the product's best and most recent attempt for individual freedom, self-determination, protection of individual rights, check & balance, a just society, a civil society, rule of law, civil rights, rule of the majority, and protection of the minority. In addition, individual freedom (or a free society) includes the freedom to pursue one's personal dreams and maximize one's personal potential without fear of oppression, resulting in jealousy, suspicious, competition, prejudice, neglect, and disparity causing the product (mankind) to be imprisoned by the pursuit of freedom.

How many times in our search for answers to many of life's situations or challenges have we looked to religions and/or religious organizations, including Judaism, Christianity, Islam, and Hinduism? The product tends to seek out religions and/or religious organizations, including Judaism, Christianity, Islam, and Hinduism for answers to many of life's situations or challenges. For example, Christianity (over centuries) has separated into many groups, groupings, organizations, and/or denominations such as Protestants, Catholic, Church of England, Disciples of Christ, Church of Nazarene, Church of God, Church of God in Christ, Episcopalian, Orthodox, Lutheran, Seven Day Adventist, Apostolic, Presbyterian, Evangelical, Methodist, Pentecostal, Baptist, Jehovah Witnesses, Latter-day Saints, Charismatic, Word of Faith, Non-denominational, Interdenominational, and World Council of Churches. Joining a religion and/or religious organizations has not solved life's situations, challenges, or difficulties. Neither will joining a sports team, club, fraternity, sorority, and/or lodge. The only

Discovering the Purpose of You, the Product

way to solve our problems, challenges, or difficulties is to seek first the manufacturer of the product (mankind).

The manufacturer designed the product (mankind) to have various types and levels of relationships (such as friends, family, marriage, and/or partnerships) that require communication including questions and opinions on various topics and subjects. The question we all should (or must) ask ourselves is, "What is our (or my) motivation (or attitude) for asking questions or seeking opinions from other people (products)?" Are we asking because we want someone (or a group) to agree with our personal agenda(s) or scheme(s)? Or are we asking for improving our individual quality of life and the quality of life of people around us? When the product asks another similar product how to operate instead of going to the manufacturer and the manufacturer's manual, the answer(s) may lead the product off course or in the wrong direction.

What happens when the product uses the wrong method to approaching situations, challenges, or difficulties? What happens when the product uses an alternate method of instructions or alternate operating procedures? When the product uses an alternate method of instructions or alternate operating procedure, malfunction will occur and lead the product off course or in the wrong direction.

What happens when the product experiments (using trial and error) with itself or with other like products instead of following the manufacturer's manual? When the product experiments (using trial and error) with itself or with another like products instead of following the manufacturer's manual, termination can occur, abuse, or a setup for the Game of Life.

The Manufacturer's Manual

Notes and Insights

Chapter 5

The Game of Life

The Manufacturer's Manual

As mentioned previously, a slave has no sense of ownership, possession, or proprietorship. A slave has no sense self-worth. A slave has no sense of self-estimation (low self-esteem). A slave has no vision. A slave has no hope. A slave hate work because he or she identify work with pain or punishment. A slave has no esteem for himself or herself because he or she has taken on the mentality of his or her master. A slave hates his brother because of low self-esteem and his brother remind him of himself. A slave has a death wish. A slave wants to leave earth. A slave is afraid to live. A slave wants to die. In addition, a slave comes into this world with two strikes against him or her and may not know or realize until it's too late.

Baseball is a game played between two teams with nine players in the field from the team that is not batting at that point. The batting team would have one person called a batter at "home plate" on the field. On a baseball field, the game is under the authority of numerous umpires. There are typically four umpires in US Major League baseball games, and up to six (and as few as one) may officiate depending on the league and the importance of the game. There are three bases numbered counterclockwise first, second, and third bases that are cushions (occasionally informally referred to as bags) shaped as 15 in (38 cm) squares which are raised a short distance above the ground. Together with home plate (the fourth base), a square is formed with sides of 90 ft. (27.4 m) called the diamond. Home plate is a pentagonal rubber slab 17 in (43.2 cm) wide *(Official Baseball Rules 2018 Edition,* Retrieved from http://mlb.mlb.com/mlb/official_info/official_rules/official_rules.jsp).

The playing field is divided into three main sections: The infield comprising of the four bases is for defensive purposes restricted by the foul lines and within the grass line (see figure). The outfield is the

Discovering the Purpose of You, the Product

grassed area outside the infield grass line between the foul lines and confined by a wall or fence. Foul territory is the complete area outside the foul lines.

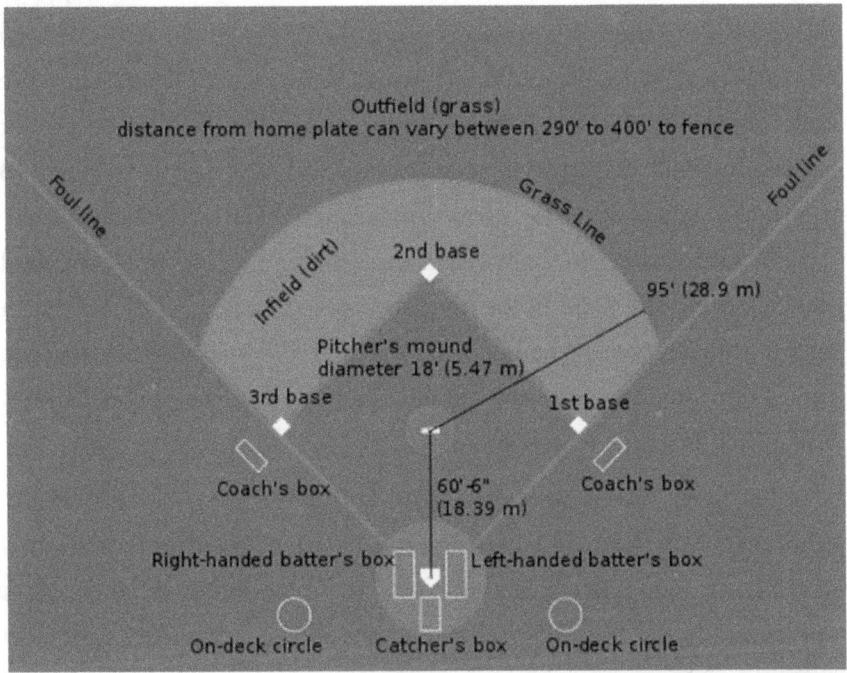

The pitcher's mound is positioned in the center of the infield. It is an 18 ft. (5.5 m) diameter mound of dirt no higher than 10 in (25.4 cm). Near the center of the mound is the pitching rubber that is a rubber slab positioned 60 ft., 6 in (18.4 m) from home plate. The pitcher must have one foot on the rubber at the start of every pitch to a batter, but the pitcher may leave the mound area once the ball is thrown (or released).

The basic contest is between the pitcher for the fielding team and the batter. The pitcher throws pitches (or throws the ball towards home plate), where the catcher for the fielding team waits (in a crouched

The Manufacturer's Manual

stance) to receive it. Behind the catcher stands the home plate umpire. The batter stands in one of the batter's boxes and tries to hit the ball with a bat (see figure above). The pitcher must keep one foot in contact with the top or front of the pitcher's rubber 24×6 in (61×15 cm) plate located on the pitcher's mound during the entire pitch. He can only take one step backward and one forward in throwing (or releasing) the ball. The catcher's job is to receive any pitches that the batter does not hit and to "call" the game by a series of hand movements to signal to the pitcher what pitch to throw and where. The catcher signals the desired location of the ball within the strike zone and in a crouched stance behind the plate holds his glove up in the desired location as a target. The catcher's role becomes more vital depending on how the game is progressing and how the pitcher responds to a given situation. Each pitch begins a new play.

The goal of the defending team is to get three members of the other team out. A player who is out must leave the field and wait for his next turn at bat. There are many ways to get batters and baserunners out including catching a batted ball in the air, tag outs, force outs, and strikeouts. After the fielding team has put out three players from the opposing team, half of the inning is over, and the team in the field and the team at bat switch places. There is no limit to the number batters that may bat in the rotation before three outs are recorded. A whole inning consists of each opposing side having an opportunity to score on offense before receiving three outs.

The goal of the team at bat is to score more runs than the opposition. A player may do so by batting, becoming a baserunner, touching all the bases in order (by one or more plays), and finally touching home plate. A player may also become a baserunner by being inserted as a pinch-runner (or substitute runner). The goal of each

Discovering the Purpose of You, the Product

batter is to enable baserunners to score or to become a baserunner himself. The batter attempts to hit the ball into fair territory (between the baselines) in such a way that the defending players cannot get them or the baserunners out. In general, the pitcher attempts to prevent this by pitching the ball in such a way that the batter cannot hit it cleanly or at all. A baserunner who has successfully touched home plate without being retired (called out) after touching all previous bases in order scores a run. In an enclosed field, a fair ball hit over the wall or fence and between the foul lines on the fly is an automatic home run, which allows the batter and all runners to touch all the bases and score. On a field with foul poles, a ball that hits a pole is also a home run. A home run hit with all bases occupied (bases loaded) is called a grand slam.

Like a batter in the game of baseball, we all must step into the batter's box (of life) and swing the bat as the ball (situations, challenges, or difficulties) comes toward home plate (in life). Imagine if you were stepping into the batter's box with two strikes against you without attempting to swing at the ball with the bat. We would consider that unfair or an unfair advantage for the pitcher or opposing team. As we are in the batter's box (of life) and attempting to swing the bat at the ball (situations, challenges, or difficulties) comes toward home plate (or life), we find ourselves somewhat off balance and trying to put (or connect) the bat to the ball in a defensive posture without hitting a ball in the air that is catchable, getting tagged out, getting forced out, and/or strikeout.

How many of us have felt like we have stepped into situations or unknown situations with two strikes against us, somewhat off balanced, without preparation, or thought we were prepared, only to find out at some later time that the situations, challenges, or difficulties went from bad to worse? I am not referring to the shame, guilt, and/or rejection

The Manufacturer's Manual

that may be associated with bad situations, challenges, or difficulties. I am referring to not reading or understanding the manufacture's manual in preparation for unknown situations, challenges, or difficulties to avoid the feelings of shame, guilt, and/or rejection leading to the malfunction and/or abuse of the product (and/or similar products). We were not designed by the manufacturer (creator) to handle the psychological and physical impact(s) resulting from shame, guilt, and/or rejection. A method is a way of approaching situations, challenges, or difficulties. What happens when the product uses the wrong method to approaching situations, challenges, or difficulties in life? Many of us approach situations, challenges, or difficulties without much preparation. How do we prepare for situations, challenges, or difficulties unknown to us? We can't avoid situations, challenges, or difficulties, but we can prepare or be prepared by seeking to pursue, study, explore, discover, understand, learn, and preoccupy oneself with the manufacturer's manual without causing further malfunction (failure and break down) and abuse (misuse and misapplication) of the product (mankind). Situations, challenges, and/or difficulties point us to the need of the manufacturer's manual leading to overcoming and subduing in our environment. The goal of the manufacturer is to transform the product (mankind) from a slavery mentality to a kingdom (fruitful, multiplying, overcoming, subduing, ruling, responsible, accountable) mentality and no longer two strikes behind upon initially stepping into the batter's box of life.

Discovering the Purpose of You, the Product

Notes and Insights

The Manufacturer's Manual

Chapter 6

Man

The Manufacturer's Manual

Who are we truly? Are we male and female? Are we a nationality or racial group? Are we Indian, American, French, Chinese, African, English, Spanish, Italian, Russian, Polish, or German? Are we an occupation such as a doctor, butcher, baker, or candlestick maker? Who truly is this being, covered by those things we think we are? This is not easy to determine, but we must turn our attention back to the origin of mankind and the original design created by the creator (or manufacturer). Our being is defined by the source of its origin. The product (mankind) is trying to define itself independent of the manufacturer, instead of defining itself dependent on the manufacturer. A baby lion is defined as such because it comes from the father and mother whom both are lions. A baby elephant is defined as such because it comes from the father and mother whom both are elephants. A baby giraffe is defined as such because it comes from the father and mother whom both are giraffes.

In the same way, the creator determined that from Him would come forth a product composed of His substance and nature. This product would have within itself the ability, authority, intelligence, wisdom, creativity, power, and all the attributes (qualities, characteristics, traits, and features) of the creator inherent to its divine genetics (or DNA - Deoxyribonucleic Acid[1]). The creator said, "Let us make this product in Our image and according to Our likeness (or resemblance)." So, the creator manufactured this product (mankind) in His own image and likeness both male and female. The creator manufactured (or fashioned) this product so that whoever or whatever looked upon this product would see or recognize the creator also. Jesus Christ came to restore that which the product lost. His work and His being reflect

---

[1] DNA is a particle that transfers the genetic instructions used (or handed down) in the growth, development, functioning, and reproduction of all known living organisms to include humans, animals, creatures, and plant life.

Discovering the Purpose of You, the Product

the identity, image, and attributes lost by the first product (Adam). The identity, image, and attributes of Jesus Christ is what answers the question of who we are truely as sons of God (or offspring). If the product (mankind) are sons of God (or offspring), then the creator is the Father. The motivation for creation was Jesus Christ because it pleased the Father to create mores sons (or offspring) that would be like His Son.

In the natural, only the father can impart identity to his children. Growing along with a true father allows (or permit) us to have a secure and firm identity to excel through life. When a father is loving, cares about his children, corrects, affirms, and teaches, the children develop (or grow) stable personalities. The person will feel secure and proud to be the child (son or daughter) of that father. The creator designed the father (or a fatherly figure) to give the offspring(s) identity. The mother, regardless of how loving, devoted, and how much she gives to her children, she can never be able to impart on them their identity because she is designed by the creator as a natural incubator (and/or companion). Change of law, policy, or regulation can't change the manufacturer's design of the product. Normally, we're given the last name of our father, and that determines our genealogy and origin, which is part of our identity and what identifies us to what family we belong. The creator is the Father of all spirits which gives us our identity and the understanding of our origin.

Our basic nature is not natural (seen), but spiritual (unseen). Before we were humans (on the seen), we were spirits (in the unseen) known and named by the creator. The creator placed (or positioned) the spirit of man (in the unseen) inside the physical body (on the seen) to operate (or function) in two realms (or dimensions) at the same time. For the spirit of man (in the unseen) and the physical body (on

The Manufacturer's Manual

the seen) to activate (or work together), the Father created the soul that would allow them to communicate and make them compatible with one another. In simple terms, man is a spirit that has a soul and lives in a physical body. In broader terms, man is a spirit that is positioned in a physical body and has a soul to process and understand the seen and the unseen realm. Man is the only product of the creator that is designed with this three-part configuration - spirit, soul, and body. Man is more than a mass made up of the head, trunk, and extremities. Man is placed in a marvelous machine called a physical body that is composed of systems and multiple organs that are interconnected. The systems include the cardiovascular system, respiratory system, digestive system, urinary system, nervous system, skeletal system, muscular system, reproductive system, immune system, and endocrine system. In addition, there is much activity occurring within the chemistry of the brain and the cells. Similarly, the spirit and the soul are composed of a series of systems and organs.

Discovering the Purpose of You, the Product

Notes and Insights

The Manufacturer's Manual

Chapter 7

Marriage (Covenant)

The Manufacturer's Manual

Within western, contemporary, modern, industrial, technological, educated society, there is a word that seems to have dropped out of common usage, sound foreign, and unfamiliar to the ears. Even among religious people, groups, and/or activities, this word has dropped out of common usage. As a result, the meaning, understanding, and action(s) of this word have been lost. In addition, a rebirth of the meaning, understanding, and action(s) of this word is needed. The word is "covenant". The concept of covenant is prominent in the manufacturer's manual. A covenant relationship is the bedrock of the manufacturer's interaction with the product (mankind). Covenant transcends (or exceed) the ever-changing whims and notions of the product (mankind). Covenant is the manufacturer's primary means of bringing stability and security into the brief and chaotic life of mankind. Covenant principles serve as the foundation for social development, government, and day to day life (or existence) of the product (mankind). A covenant is typically formed upon several promises grouped together for a specific purpose. In addition, the covenant reveals the purpose. The manufacturer initiated a covenant with the product (mankind) that includes promises, terms, conditions of the agreement, and a sign of the covenant in the form of a sacrifice. A covenant is a binding agreement finalized, confirmed, or settled by a sacrifice, making a genuine commitment between two or more parties in the relationship. A sacrifice is a life laid down for another person or cause. Throughout history, the penalty for breaking a covenant was imprisonment or death. Today, in certain cultures the penalty for breaking a covenant is imprisonment or death. A covenant is an unbreakable, immutable, unalterable agreement between two or parties. Marriage is a sign of a covenant in the form of a life laid down for the other person.

Discovering the Purpose of You, the Product

Marriage is a covenant relationship designed by the creator. Marriage is what the creator uses as a sign (or picture) to help the mankind understand covenant. Marriage is a life laid down for the other person in a covenant relationship. Contrary to contemporary beliefs, the manufacturer does not send the male (product) a mate. In one way or another, the manufacturer displays to the male, females for choosing a suitable wife. The male chooses a mate (or wife to be) and extends an invitation to a covenant relationship. The female (product) chooses to accept his invitation. The manufacturer designed the female (product) to be chased by the male (product) all the days of her life.

The ideal preparation of marriage may be an arranged marriage orchestrated by the fathers of the groom and bride. The male (product) asks his father for a female (product) hand in marriage. His father talks with the female's father. Once an agreement is finalized, preparations for the marriage in the form of an engagement begin (not preparations for the marriage ceremony). An engagement can be carried out for 1 to 3 years. An engagement is a time of preparation for the groom and the bride. Preparation may include building a house, locating a suitable occupation, building a business, completing education requirements, hunting, fishing, farming, and/or domestication training, including cooking, cleaning, sewing, and hygiene. The amount of time for an engagement may be determined by many factors or considerations, including the availability of the necessary resources needed beyond the actual wedding ceremony and domestication training (or exposure) received prior to the engagement. An ideal situation would be the fathers (or fatherly figures) in a community would work together and lead a series of coordinated efforts in making the necessary preparations for life's situations, challenges, or difficulties after the wedding ceremony. In addition, what is gained during the engagement

The Manufacturer's Manual

is primarily for the protection of the bride (or wife) after the wedding ceremony. The woman he is looking for does not exist. She is in his head. She is not what you want her to be. She is what you make her to be. His work is to take the raw material he married and cultivate her into the woman in his head, presenting her to himself. To cultivate the raw material into a woman, the male (product) must stay linked to the manufacturer and not operate independently.

"The woman, good for the man." The female is the manufacturer's idea. A woman is designed by the creator as a natural incubator. An incubator is a device used to grow and maintain microbiological, biological, molecule, or cell structures. An incubator can sustain optimum temperature, humidity, and other conditions such as the carbon dioxide (CO_2) and oxygen content of the atmosphere inside. Incubators aid in a variety of functions in a scientific laboratory. Shaking incubators integrate movement to blend cultures. Gas incubators regulate (or control) the internal vapor (or air) composition. Some incubators have a means of circulating the air inside of them to safeguard unfluctuating distribution of temperatures. Incubators can be built for laboratory use with a redundant power source to safeguard that power outages do not disrupt experiments or tests. Incubators are made in a variety of sizes, including tabletop models for premature infants and warm rooms for large numbers of samples. An incubator is a helper of life.

A female (whether single or married) is a natural incubator (or helper). Her whole body is incubation. An incubator can bring life to everything. Whatever you give to an incubator, it will give life and give it back to you. Whatever you give to an incubator, it will multiply and give it back to you. The female (product) of mankind must be careful of who and what they listen to because she can incubate what

Discovering the Purpose of You, the Product

she receives in her ears (and her womb). A female produces what she keeps listening to. If you give her a word, she will give you a sentence. If you give her a sentence, she will give you a paragraph. If you give her a paragraph, she will give you a chapter. If you give her a chapter, she will give you a book. If you give her sperm, she will give life, multiply it, and give you a baby. If you give her a house, she will give you a home. If you give her food, she will give you a meal. If you give her frustration, she will give you hell. A female will never keep anything. A female may hold it for some time but eventually, give it back. It will not come back the same way you gave it. If the manufacturer created (or designed) the female (product) as an incubator (or helper of life), the female has the ability the help the male (product) become better. Help the manufacturer help the male (product) to become. The female (product) should not try to be equal to the male (product) independent of the manufacturer's direction. In addition, the female (product) should not try to be equal to the male (product) on her own terms which may develop into unintended consequences in the lives of the offspring(s).

Marriage has incredible benefits that we really don't realize. Each partner has a strength that the other does not have. In marriage, one idea can complete the other idea. In marriage, one idea can complete than the other idea. Marriage forces us to make better choices. Marriage provides an opportunity to be a better self. The woman is good for the man in a covenant relationship. In addition, the man is good for the woman in a covenant relationship. In many relationships, both the male and female are unaware that they are good for one another unless both the male and female are dependent on the manufacturer for guidance or help. The male (product) was created by the manufacturer to generate (or produce) what he desires from the resources around him. The male is designed to be the protector of

The Manufacturer's Manual

everything place under his care. The male is designed with a stronger bone frame and bigger muscles mass (not for abuse), but to guard and protect the woman, children, and the environment. In addition, the female (product) was not created for manipulation, intimidation, and/or domination. Guarding and protecting conveys rule (regulate), order (protocol, direction), and structure (foundation, assembly) into an environment (or surroundings) eliminating chaos, confusion, and violence resulting in security, peace, and prosperity.

Discovering the Purpose of You, the Product

Notes and Insights

The Manufacturer's Manual

Chapter 8

Maintaining the Product

The Manufacturer's Manual

When we purchase a vehicle, we bring it home with excitement and enthusiasms. Most of the time, a set of instructions or manual comes with the vehicle. The set of instructions or the manual is placed in such a way that when we open the vehicle, we can reach for it easily, or placed in the storage compartment. The manufacturer of the vehicle wants all those using the vehicle to see the set of instructions or manual before attempting to drive the vehicle. For example:

- "Warning – Before driving your vehicle, please read this."

- "Don't attempt to use or operate this vehicle without reading the manual."

- "This will ensure familiarity with controls and maintenance requirements assisting you in the safe operation of your vehicle."

Most of us don't observe the warning(s). We drive the vehicle without reading the manual. This can open the door to experimenting (trial and error) without guidance, direction and/or controls (or boundaries) causing malfunction (failure or break down) and abuse (misuse or misapplication). Included in the set of instructions or the manual are three types of vehicle maintenance processes needed to allow the vehicle to safely operate as designed by the manufacturer.

- Preventive Maintenance

- Repairable Maintenance

- Deferred Maintenance

Preventive Maintenance is the periodic upkeep or care required for proper operation of the product throughout its existence including

Discovering the Purpose of You, the Product

manufacturer's upgrade(s). The periodic upkeep or care of a vehicle can include oil & oil filter change every 3000 miles, tire rotation every 15,000 miles, and various checks of components including air filter, fuel filter, and rubber hoses for cracks & leaks. Repairable Maintenance is the process of restoring the product to proper operation including manufacturer's recall(s) caused by defect(s). The restoring of a vehicle can include repairs and replacements of parts needed to operate a vehicle safely including starter, battery, and alternator. Deferred Maintenance is postponing of Preventive Maintenance and Repairable Maintenance for a later time because of the non-availability of funds, replacement parts, and/or time. The manufacturer has built into His product the DNA needed for Preventive Maintenance, Repairable Maintenance, and Deferred Maintenance.

Periodic upkeep or care (Preventive Maintenance) for proper operation of the product can include consuming healthy foods, participating in regular physical activity every day, and the words we speak and hear. The process of restoring (Repairable Maintenance) the product to proper operation is like what we would do to a vehicle if it is not operating sufficiently. Suppose you are driving a vehicle on the road, then it would not accelerate (when needed) or it began to slow down without pressing or pushing on the brake with your foot. You pull over on the side of the road and realize the engine is not operating to its full potential. What do you do? The vehicle is drivable but does not accelerate to its full potential while in traffic. You have one of two choices. Continue to drive vehicle as-is or take the vehicle to a certified automobile mechanic? You can postpone (or defer) the maintenance because of non-availability of funds, replacement parts, and/or time.

The Manufacturer's Manual

Have you ever postpone required repairable maintenance needed in your life? Have you ever recurrently driven on the road of life without repair(s)? Have you ever driven on the road (of life), slowing the flow of traffic (or others' lives) behind you because of the lack of needed repairs on your vehicle (or in your life)? Sometimes (and probably more often than willing to admit), we need to get off the road of life and take our situations, challenges, or difficulties to the manufacturer for repairs so we can be restored back to full operation. Sometimes we continue to operate without needed repair(s) because of stubbornness, fear, and/or ignorance causing problems. Maybe, therefore we (the product) continue to have problems with sexual misconduct issues such as sexual harassment, molestation, and adultery. At some point (preferably in early stages), the product has need of help (to reach out to the manufacturer) before the product is out of control causing more unnecessary damage to itself and to other products.

Discovering the Purpose of You, the Product

Notes and Insights

The Manufacturer's Manual

Chapter 9

Meal(s) and Water

The Manufacturer's Manual

For a vehicle to operate according to the manufacturer's specification and full potential, the vehicle will need fuel (petroleum). Fuel, engine oil, brake fluid, power steering fluid, engine coolant and transmission fluid is needed to operate a vehicle. The movement and routing of fluids (including fuel, engine oil, brake fluid, power steering fluid, engine coolant, and transmission fluid) throughout the engine (and transmission) is controlled by internal systems' components. The systems that control the movement and routing of fluids include the oil system, brake system, power steering system, and engine coolant system. Each system has individual components and hoses (or connectors) that allow the movement of fluid throughout the engine (and transmission). Like a vehicle that needs fuel (with air and fire) to operate, the physical body needs fuel called food to consume to operate.

As mentioned earlier, the physical body is composed of systems including the cardiovascular system, respiratory system, digestive system, urinary system, nervous system, skeletal system, muscular system, reproductive system, immune system, endocrine system, brain, and cells. Each system within the physical body works together in a coordinated effort to convert food (that is consumed) into usable material for energy, building, and repair. The manufacturer placed a multitude of solid foods (including water) in the product's surroundings (or environment). The food we consume is the Manufacturer's medicine for the physical body. These foods can be classified as vegetables, fruits, nuts, seeds, grains, meats, and fish. The conversion of food into usable material is called digestion. Digestion is the breakdown of food into a usable material called nutrients for absorption and assimilation into the physical body. Nutrients are divided into six basic groups: water, proteins, carbohydrates, fat, vitamins, and minerals. Water is used to dissolve and transport nutrients, remove waste products, and regulate

Discovering the Purpose of You, the Product

body temperature. Proteins are used to build new tissue, antibodies, enzymes, and hormones. Carbohydrates are used to provide energy. Fats are used to deliver long-term energy as well as for insulation and protection. Vitamins are used to facilitate the use of other nutrients, regulate growth, and manufacture hormones. Minerals are used to aid in building bones and teeth, in muscle functions, and in nervous system activities.

The physical body is a brilliant design. The physical body does not have a water storage system like a camel which is why they are known as ships of the desert. We constantly must drink water to replace the water we have lost, but the body does have a Water Recycling System and a Drought Management System to help dissolve and transport nutrients, remove waste products, and regulate body temperature. Our bodies consist of approximately 70% water. We need to ensure that this balance is maintained as every single cell in our body needs water to help absorb the nutrients. We lose water constantly because when it is hot, we sweat, perspire, or secrete. When we do physical activity, we breathe, urinate, cry, cough, and sneeze. Because we do not have a water storage system and are always losing water, we need to regularly drink water to replace that which we have lost.

Are you aware that your body has a water recycling system? The human body is the finest recycling machine. When we drink water or consume water from fruits and vegetables, the body recycles it to the tune of hundreds of liters per day to maintain natural human functions, including building, repair, and waste disposal. Without fresh supplies of drinking water, our bodies are unable to transport nutrients and blood plasma to where needed, and we will soon become fatigued both mentally and physically. Should this happen, the Human Body's Drought Management System turns on and endeavors to prevent respiratory water loss by creating histamines[2] which shut off the capillaries in your lungs. This restriction reduces water loss from breathing and makes breathing very difficult. It may seem like we are really struggling to breathe. The body is making this occur on purpose to save the brain from damage due to a lack of water. When this happens, drinking water as soon as possible will bring back the capillaries to normal size and rehydrate the brain.

The digestive system consists of the gastrointestinal tract plus the additional organs of digestion (the tongue, salivary glands, pancreas, liver, and gallbladder) to break down foods, absorb the nutrients, and eliminate waste products. The consumption of water is used to facilitate (simplify, smooth, or help) the breakdown of foods, absorption of nutrients, and elimination of waste products. In this system, the process of digestion has many stages, starting in the mouth and ending in the large intestine where the solid waste products of digestion (feces) are eliminated from the anus through the rectum. In addition, the urinary system consisting of the kidneys, adrenal gland, ureters, bladder eliminates waste (urine) from the body through the urethra.

---

[2]Histamine is an organic nitrogenous compound involved in local immune responses, regulating biological function in the stomach, and acting as a neurotransmitter for the brain, spinal cord, and uterus (or womb). Histamine can be noticed as mucus in a runny noise upon an infection or part of cold symptoms.

Discovering the Purpose of You, the Product

Notes and Insights

The Manufacturer's Manual

Chapter 10

Medicine

The Manufacturer's Manual

In simple terms, a disease (or infirmity) is a dis-ease (or discomfort) in the physical body caused by misuse or abuse, intentionally or unintentionally. What seems like discomfort is the body's way of protecting itself from further infection (or damage) to bring about healing (or repair). For example, the body's defense against the "common cold" is the buildup of mucus (from white blood cells[3]) in the nostrils and/or throat areas to fight against infection. The physical body's systems (composed of the cardiovascular system, respiratory system, digestive system, urinary system, nervous system, skeletal system, muscular system, reproductive system, immune system, endocrine system, brain, and cells) work together in a coordinated effort to convert food and water (that is consumed) into usable material for energy, building, and repair (including preventative medicine). The manufacturer's instructions are health to all our flesh, including the leaves of trees. They are for healing for the nations. The product (mankind) is attempting to solve or fix its health problems independent of the manufacturer. Dis-ease is caused by the lack of knowledge rooted in darkness (or the absence of light) because of attempting to operate independently of the manufacturer. In addition, an addiction is a manifestation of a dis-ease left untreated (or not addressed) over a period of time.

As mentioned previously, water is used to dissolve and transport nutrients, remove waste products, and regulate body temperature. In addition, water is the lubricant of the physical body. The manufacturer did not provide (or create) a substitution. Unfortunately, the product's (man-made) fluids, like carbonated drinks (commonly known as soda),

---

[3] White blood cells are the cells of the immune system that are involved in protecting the body against infectious disease and foreign invaders.

Discovering the Purpose of You, the Product

teas, coffees, and sugar-flavored drinks, are not adequate substitutes for water. These fluids add to the dehydration of the physical body. Lack of water causes dehydration, leading to the possibilities of heartburn, arthritis, back pain, angina, migraines, colitis, asthma, high blood pressure, early adult-onset diabetes, and/or high cholesterol levels (Batmanghelidj, F MD, *Your Body's Many Cries for Water*).

Water avoids and helps to remedy heartburn (dis-ease). Heartburn is a signal of water deficiency in the upper part of the gastrointestinal tract and a key thirst signal of the human body. The use of antacids or tablet medications in the treatment of this discomfort does not correct dehydration, and the body continues to suffer because of its water deficiency. Not distinguishing heartburn as a sign of dehydration will over a period produce inflammation of the stomach and duodenum[4], hiatal hernia[5], ulceration, and sooner or later, cancers in the gastrointestinal tract, liver, and pancreas.

Water avoids and helps to remedy arthritis (dis-ease). Rheumatoid joint pain (also known as arthritis) is a signal of water deficiency in the painful joint. Arthritis can affect the young as well as the old. The use of painkillers and/or medications does not remedy the problem but exposes the person to further damage.

Water avoids and helps to remedy back pain (dis-ease). Low back pain and Ankylosing Spondylitis[6] arthritis of the spine are signs of water deficiency in the spinal column and discs (cartilage). The discs

---

[4] The duodenum is the first section and short portion of the small intestine connected to the stomach. It is about 10 inches (25 cm) long, while the entire small intestine measures about 20 feet (6.5 meters).

[5] A hiatal hernia occurs (or happens) when part of the stomach pushes upward through the diaphragm. The diaphragm normally has a small opening (hiatus) through which the food tube (esophagus) passes on its way connected to the stomach. The stomach can push up through this opening and cause a hiatal hernia.

6 Ankylosing spondylitis (AS) is a type of arthritis caused by long term inflammation of the joints of the spine.

The Manufacturer's Manual

are like cushions composed of material and water that support the weight of the body. Low back pain and Ankylosing Spondylitis can be treated with increased water intake and a decrease in fluids that cause dehydration. Not distinguishing arthritis and low back pain as signs of dehydration in the joints and treating them with painkillers, pain medications, acupuncture[7], and ultimately surgery will over a period produce osteoarthritis[8] that may lead to deformity of the spine and limbs. In addition, pain medications used over a period of time have their own life-threatening complications.

Water avoids and helps to remedy angina (dis-ease). Heart pain (also known as angina) is a sign of water deficiency in the heart-lung axis. Angina can be treated with increased water intake until the patient is free of pain and independent of medications. Medical supervision is practical, sensible, and wise. However, increased water intake is angina's remedy.

Water avoids and helps to remedy migraines (dis-ease). A migraine headache is a sign of water deficiency by the brain and the eyes. A migraine headache can clear up if dehydration is prevented from establishing in the body. Dehydration that causes migraine headaches might sooner or later cause inflammation of the back of the eye and perhaps the loss of eyesight.

Water avoids and helps to remedy colitis (dis-ease). Colitis pain is a signal of water deficiency in the large intestine. Colitis pain is associated with constipation because the large intestine constricts to squeeze the last drop of water from the feces (thus the lack of water for lubrication). Not distinguishing colitis pain as a sign of dehydration can cause persistent constipation. Later in life, it can cause fecal

---

[7] Acupuncture is a form of alternative medicine in which thin needles are inserted into the body.

[8] Osteoarthritis (OA) is a type of joint disease that results from breakdown of joint cartilage and bone.

Discovering the Purpose of You, the Product

impacting leading to diverticulitis[9], hemorrhoids, polyps[10], and could increase the possibility of developing cancer of the colon and rectum (Batmanghelidj, F MD, *Your Body's Many Cries for Water*, Page 34)

Water (and salt) avoid and help to remedy asthma (dis-ease). Asthma is an inflammatory disease of the airways of the lungs. The lungs are the primary organs of the respiratory system. Their function in the respiratory system is to extract oxygen from the atmosphere, transfer oxygen into the bloodstream, and to release carbon dioxide from the bloodstream into the atmosphere in the form of vapor in the process of gas exchange (What is *Asthma*, https://www.webmd.com/asthma/guide/what-is-asthma#1). Asthma is characterized by recurrent episodes of wheezing, shortness of breath, chest tightness, coughing, reversible airflow obstruction, and bronchospasm. Asthma is a complication of dehydration in the body. Asthma is caused by the human body's drought management system. In asthma, free passage of air is obstructed so that water does not leave the body in the form of vapor (the winter steam when breathing out during very cold conditions). Increased water intake will prevent asthma attacks. Asthmatics consume more salt to break the mucus plugs in the lungs that obstruct the free flow of air in and out of the air sacs (alveoli). Not distinguishing asthma as the indicator of dehydration in the body of a growing child can allow for irreversible genetic damage (Batmanghelidj, F MD, Your Body's Many Cries for Water, Page 113)

Water avoids and helps to remedy high blood pressure (also known as hypertension). Hypertension (dis-ease) is a state of adaptation of the body to a generalized drought when there is not enough water to fill all the blood vessels that distribute water into vital cells. Through a

---

[9] Diverticulitis is a gastrointestinal disease due to abnormal pouches which developed in the wall of the large intestine that has become inflamed.

[10] A polyp is an abnormal growth of tissue projecting from a mucus membrane.

The Manufacturer's Manual

process called reverse osmosis, water from the blood serum[11] is filtered and injected into important cells through tiny holes in their membranes. Extra pressure is needed for the injection process. Like injecting an IV (intravenous) with water in hospitals, the body injects water into tens of trillions of cells all at the same time. Water and some salt intake will bring blood pressure back to normal. Not distinguishing hypertension as one of the major indicators of dehydration in the human body and treating it with diuretics[12] that further dehydrate the body can cause blockage by cholesterol of the heart arteries and the arteries that lead to the brain. This can cause heart attacks and small or massive strokes that paralyze. Sooner or later this can cause kidney disease. It can also cause brain damage and neurological disorders like Alzheimer's disease.

Water avoids and helps to remedy early adult-onset diabetes (dis-ease). Adult-onset diabetes is another adaptive state to severe dehydration of the human body (Batmanghelidj, F MD, *Your Body's Many Cries for Water*, Page 123). To have adequate water in circulation and for the brain's priority water needs to be met, the release of insulin is inhibited to prevent insulin from pushing water into all body cells. In diabetes, few cells get survival rations of water. Water and some salt will reverse adult-onset diabetes in its early stages. Not recognizing adult-onset diabetes as a complication of dehydration can (over a period) cause massive damage to the blood vessels all over the body. This can cause loss of the toes, feet, and legs from gangrene. This can cause eye damage and blindness.

---

[11] Serum is the component that is neither a blood cell (serum does not contain white or red blood cells) nor a clotting factor. Serum is the blood plasma not including the fibrinogens. Serum includes all proteins not used in blood clotting (coagulation), all the electrolytes, antibodies, antigens, hormones, and any exogenous substances (e.g., drugs and microorganisms).

[12] A diuretic is any substance that promotes the increased production of urine.

Discovering the Purpose of You, the Product

Water helps to avoid high blood cholesterol (dis-ease) and aids in lowering cholesterol levels. High cholesterol levels are an indicator of the body's drought management system activating. Cholesterol is a waxy substance that is in the gaps of some cell membranes to safeguard them against losing their vital water content during osmosis[13]. Cholesterol is used to manufacture nerve cell membranes and hormones and is also used as a protection against water deficiency of other vital cells that would normally exchange water through their cell membranes.

The physical body is a brilliantly designed product consisting of approximately 70% water. We need to safeguard this balance. Exposure to temperatures of 120 degrees whiles living in the Middle East helped my understanding of the importance of water to the human body. Every single cell in our body needs water to help absorb nutrients. We constantly must drink water to replace the water we have lost to facilitate (simplify, smooth, or help) the breakdown of foods, absorption of nutrients, and elimination of waste products from the physical body.

- Water facilitates digestion and/or the breakdown of foods for energy, building, and repair.

- Water allows the cells to absorb nutrients needed from the breakdown of foods.

- Water allows waste and toxins to be eliminated from the physical body quicker and easier.

- Water is the lubricant of the physical body.

---

[13] Osmosis is the tendency of a fluid, usually water, to pass through a semipermeable membrane into a solution where the solvent concentration is higher, thus equalizing the concentrations of materials on either side of the membrane.

The Manufacturer's Manual

The physical body is a marvelous machine created by the manufacturer as a house for man. Our well-being must be understood from the manufacturer (or creator), or inside out instead of from the outside in. We are spiritual beings first housed in a physical body. The physical body is composed of systems, including the cardiovascular system, respiratory system, digestive system, urinary system, nervous system, skeletal system, muscular system, reproductive system, immune system, endocrine system, brain, and cells. The manufacturer placed a multitude of nutrients in the form of solid foods and water in the product's surroundings (or environment) for energy, building, and repair. Each system within the physical body works collectively in a coordinated effort to convert food (that is consumed) into usable material for energy, building, and repair to help cure dis-ease (or discomfort). Dis-ease is caused by the lack of knowledge rooted in darkness (or the absence of light). Lack of knowledge caused by remaining independent of the manufacturer has caused the product (mankind) to not solve or fix its health problems. The manufacturer's manual is health to all our flesh, including the leaves of trees which are for the healing of the nations. The manufacturer's manual is like medicine to all our flesh, bringing deliverance, healing, and peace from the inside out.

Discovering the Purpose of You, the Product

Notes and Insights

The Manufacturer's Manual

Chapter 11

Money

The Manufacturer's Manual

The manufacturer (or creator) made all people. Some are rich; some are poor depending on what and how they see. Money can be a terrible taskmaster, but a wonderful servant. Seek first the manufacturer's ways of operating, and everything you need will be added to you. He will supply your needs.

What happens when the product does not give priority above everything to seeking the manufacturer (creator of the money), the origin of money, the nature of money, the purpose money, and the economy of money in the manufacturer's manual? What happens when the product tries to operate or solve problems independent of the manufacture's manual? What happens when we ask another person how to operate (or use money) instead of focusing on the manufacturer and the manufacturer's manual? What happens when we use the wrong method to approach the use of money (in situations, challenges, or difficulties in life)? What happens when we use an alternate method of instructions or operations for the use money? What happens when we experiment (using trial and error) with money instead of following the manufacturer's manual?

What happens when we do not give priority above everything to seeking the manufacturer (creator of money), the origin of money, the nature money, the purpose money, and the economy money in the manufacturer's manual? Priority (above all others, highest valve, or above everything) indicate there are other priorities that preoccupy our time, energy, creativity, and resources, not allowing us (the product) to focus on important endeavors or activities. The manufacture's manual indicates or directs us to seek first the manufacturer and right positioning or alignment. If we are not in right positioning or alignment with the manufacturer, then abuse of money is inevitable, unavoidable, predictable, and/or foreseeable.

Discovering the Purpose of You, the Product

What happens when we try to operate or solve (financial) problems independent of the manufacturer's manual? When we try to operate or solve (financial) problems independent of the manufacturer's manual, there is no communication (or very little communication) between the manufacturer and us about the use of money. Malfunction can occur. Abuse is inevitable, and/or potential is wasted or lost.

What happens when we ask another person (or group) how to operate instead of going to the manufacturer and the manufacturer's manual? How many times have we asked those around us their opinion on an issue or subject, including friends, educators, and/or medical professionals? How many times in our search for answers to many of life's situations or challenges have we looked to a variety of human governmental systems, including feudalism, imperialism, colonialism, communism, socialism, dictatorship, and democracy to solve financial issues?

There are multiple ways the manufacturer will add to His product or provide for His product as the product continues to seek the manufacturer first. The manufacturer's manual mentioned several ways the manufacturer added to or provided for His product (mankind) through instructions, directions, wisdom, and/or obedience throughout history.

- Joseph saved 1/5 of grain produced for 7 years (Book of Genesis, chapter 41).

- Moses got water from a rock (Book of Exodus, chapter 17).

- The children of Israel received manna from Heaven *(Book of Exodus,* chapter 16).

The Manufacturer's Manual

- God gives us the power and ability to create or get wealth (*Book of Deuteronomy,* chapter 8).

- The widow fed Elijah her last meal and then received multiple barrels of oil and meal (*Book of I Kings,* chapter 17).

- Elijah was fed by the ravens (Book of I Kings, chapter 17).

- Bring Tithes and Offerings into His storehouse, so there will be substance in His house, and the windows of Heaven will open (*Book of Malachi,* chapter 3).

- Jesus Christ instructed experienced fishermen to throw the net on the other side of the boat (*Book of John,* chapter 21).

- Jesus Christ instructed the disciples to take money from the fish's mouth to pay taxes (*Book of Matthew,* chapter 17).

- Jesus Christ was motivated by compassion to feed the multitude that followed him (five thousand) with five loaves of bread and two fishes because of their distress (*Book of Matthew,* chapter 14).

- After following Him for three days, Jesus Christ was motivated by compassion to feed the multitude (four thousand) with seven loaves of bread and few little fishes because of them continue to follow Him for three days without eating (*Book of Matthew,* chapter 16).

- The good and faithful servants produced twice the amount of their talents (from five & two talents) and received a just (or fair) reward, but the unprofitable servant with one talent who did not produce twice the amount or with interest was punished and cast out. The manufacturer has designed

Discovering the Purpose of You, the Product

the product with the capability to give back a return on the investment (*Book of Matthew,* chapter 25).

- Man ought always to pray and not faint, and the creator will avenge His product that cries day and night unto Him with determination (*Book of Luke,* chapter 18).

- They had all things in common, sold possessions, brought monies, and laid monies at the apostles' feet. They distributed the money to many according to their need (*Book of Acts,* chapter 2).

- The Philippians gave unto Paul not of necessity, but so that fruit would abound to their account providing an odor of sweet smell, a sacrifice acceptable, and well pleasing to the creator (Father). As a result, God will supply all their needs according to His riches in glory by Christ Jesus (*Book of Philippians,* chapter 4).

- Give, and it will be given unto you: money, resources, and/or favor (*Book of Luke,* chapter 6).

The listing above is not an inclusive (or complete) list but gives the product (mankind) an assurance that the manufacturer (Father) is faithful to His product throughout the product's existence (or history). Seek first the manufacturer's method of operation and His right positioning, and everything you need (including money, resources, and/or favor) will be added or follow you.

The Manufacturer's Manual

Notes and Insights

Chapter 12

Making of a Disciple
(Missing Link to Maturity)

The Manufacturer's Manual

Within western, contemporary, modern, industrial, technological, educated society, there is a word that seems to have dropped out of common usage. It sounds foreign and unfamiliar to the ears. Even among religious people, groups, and/or activities, this action (and result) has dropped out of common usage. As a result, the meaning and understanding of this action (and result) have been lost. In addition, a rebirth of the meaning, understanding, and action(s) of this word is much needed. The word is "disciple (or discipleship)." The concept, actions, or results of discipleship is prominent in the manufacturer's manual. The purpose of the making of a disciple (or discipleship) is to help the disciple (or protégé) to grow up (mature), grow out (of negative character flaws or deficiencies), and grow into (the creator's or manufacturer's intentions). In addition, the disciple should always help disciple others regardless of their maturity level. The disciple should always have (or be exposed to) someone of greater maturity and someone of lesser maturity. Discipleship brings out the manufacturer's intention for the product.

What is the manufacturer's intention for His product and creation? The creator said, "Let us make this product in our image and according to Our likeness (or resemblance)." So, the creator manufactured this product (mankind) in His own image and likeness as both male and female. The creator manufactured (or fashioned) this product so that whoever or whatever looked upon this product would see and recognize the creator also. Jesus Christ came to restore that which the product lost. His work and His being reflect the identity, image, and attributes lost by the first product (Adam). The identity, image, and attributes of Jesus Christ is what answers the question of who we are truely as sons of God (or offsprings). If the product (mankind) are sons of God (or offspring), then the creator is the Father. The

Discovering the Purpose of You, the Product

motivation for creation was Jesus Christ because it pleased the Father to create mores sons (or offspring) that would be like His Son.

Discipleship is defined as the process of duplication (or reproduction) in the life of the disciple who has submitted himself or herself to a more mature disciple (or leader) for training and development. The mature disciple (or leader) models their life before the attentive and inquisitive eyes of the younger (or less mature) disciple (or student), so that the patterns of behavior, coping methods, and philosophies can be imparted and followed by the student. The disciple takes the posture of a servant, then performs menial tasks as an apprentice. During the learning process, the apprentice is exposed to principles and assimilated truths that only can be absorbed through observation. Servanthood is often misconstrued as a negative coercion rather the positive path to completeness, promotion, and/or success that it was initially designed to accomplish. Because of the abuse and misuse that has been suffered by many races, including the Native American Indians and the African Americans, the thought of serving another person usually is despised and rebelled against. The manufacturer's manual frequently refers to discipleship as a place or position to help bring about completeness, promotion, and/or success and as the vehicle to help the disciple (or protégé) to grow up (mature), grow out (of negative character flaws or deficiencies), and grow into (the creator's or manufacturer's intentions). There are many products who we may call successful (on the outside), but still exist with hidden character flaws or deficiencies that cause problems for themselves and our society. They need discipleship.

There are multiple ways a person can be discipled by another person as both persons continue to seek the manufacturer first. The manufacturer's manual mentioned several people as examples of

The Manufacturer's Manual

discipleship, and the help given to the next generation(s) through instructions, directions, wisdom, and/or obedience.

- Abraham, Issacs, and Jacob (Israel)
- Pharaoh and Joseph
- Jethro (father-in-law) and Moses
- Moses and Joshua
- Elijah and Elisha
- Eli and Samuel
- Samuel and Saul
- Saul and David
- Jonathan and David
- Samuel and David
- Nathan and David
- David (father) and Solomon (son)
- Naomi (mother-in-law) and Ruth
- Mordecai (cousin) and Esther
- The Father and His Son (Jesus Christ)
- Jesus Christ and the Disciples
- Barabbas and Paul
- Paul and Timothy

Discovering the Purpose of You, the Product

- Paul and Titus

The listing above is not an inclusive (or complete) list but gives the product (mankind) an assurance that the creator (Father) is faithful to His product throughout the product's growth (or development). The elder (mature) disciple will teach and model to the younger disciple how to conduct themselves publicly and privately. Mentoring and/or coaching is not a substitute for the making of a disciple. There are elements of mentoring and/or coaching in the process of making a disciple, but mentoring and/or coaching is not a substitute. The making of a disciple involves the leader pouring their life into the disciple, therefore transferring his or her spirit (heart) or committing to the faithful ones the task (or duty) of overseeing the mysteries of the Kingdom of God (or the manufacturer's intent) to this generation and the generations to come.

The Manufacturer's Manual

Notes and Insights

Chapter 13

Ministry (Office)

The Manufacturer's Manual

The models of Ministry in contemporary modern-day society and modern-day churches are incomplete. In addition, the models of assembly in contemporary modern-day society and modern-day churches are incomplete. "We have one leader and many churches, instead of many leaders and one Church" (Prince, Derek, 1971, Five Main Ministries CDMM1). The participation in "Sunday School", "Children's Church", "Children's Ministry" and/or the "Mega Church" is not a substitute for the ongoing care of a pastor along with assembling with believers in an ordinary and active way that is motivated by concern, compassion, and empathy for humanity. Jesus Christ did not come to establish a religion or an organization. He came to bring back (or restore) what mankind lost in the Garden of Eden. Mankind lost dominion and the connection to the creator (or manufacturer). Mankind was no longer dependent on the creator but became independent of the creator. No longer a king, but a slave. A slave has no sense of ownership, possession, or proprietorship. A slave has no sense self-worth. A slave has no sense of self-estimation (low self-esteem). A slave has no vision. A slave has no hope. A slave hates work because he or she identifies work with pain or punishment. A slave has no esteem for himself or herself because he or she has taken on the mentality of his or her master. A slave hates his brother because of low self-esteem and his brother reminds him of himself. A slave has a death wish. A slave wants to leave earth. A slave is afraid to live. A slave wants to die. Slavery and the results, consequences, or outcomes are really the unfoldings of the product's attempt to operate and experiment independently of the creator (or manufacturer). Jesus Christ came to bring back (or restore) the product (mankind) from a slavery mentality to a dominion (fruitful, multiplying, overcoming, subduing, ruling, responsible, accountable) mentality through the process of making disciples. In addition, Jesus Christ came to

Discovering the Purpose of You, the Product

reconnect mankind back to the creator (or manufacturer). Woe to the land, when the slave (or child) becomes king. The slave (or child) needs a tutor. Discipleship is designed to turn the slave back into a king (or son of God).

Discipleship involves the leader pouring their life into the disciple, therefore transferring his or her heart or committing to the faithful ones the task (or duty) of overseeing the mysteries of the Kingdom of God as leaders in a respective office(s) of ministry, including apostles, prophets, teachers, pastors (shepherds, elders, bishops), evangelists, and deacons (helpers) operating in the local church. Are we building the Kingdom of God in the hearts and/or minds of people or are we building our own little kingdoms(or local churches? The local church is not a building. The local church is a people within a given area (with no overlapping) that is led by pastors, shepherds, bishops and/or elders undertaking the shepherd's work. The shepherd's work includes:

- A life laid down
- To know and be known
- To speak and lead
- To feed
- To protect
- To search out
- To gather the dispersed
- To proclaim deliverance to the captive
- To bound up the hurting

The Manufacturer's Manual

- To heal the broken-hearted
- To recover the sight to the blind
- To set at liberty those who are bruised
- To strengthen the weak
- To guide those who are directionless
- To carry the broken until they are strong enough to carry themselves
- To restore those who are tired
- To bring comfort
- To prepare a table with nourishment
- To anoint those in need
- To proclaim the acceptable year of the creator

In addition, the local church is the final court of appeals for:

- Disputes between believers
- Doctrine
- Moral Conduct

The local church is the womb and/or incubator that facilitates the development (or maturing) of people operating in miracles, gifts of healing, helps, governments, and diversities of tongues, producing mature persons (or sons of God) capable of handling the mysteries of the Kingdom of God and who will become deacons, apostles, prophets, teachers, evangelists, and/or leaders in their respective areas of expertise throughout the land.

Discovering the Purpose of You, the Product

Notes and Insights

The Manufacturer's Manual

Chapter 14

Music

The Manufacturer's Manual

Music is a creation of the manufacturer's nature, beauty, and love. The manufacturer created a product (cherubim or angel) with components (or features) of beauty including sardius, topaz, diamond, beryl, onyx, jasper, sapphire, emerald, carbuncle, gold, tablets, and pipes as an expression of His nature and love to all creation. The product (cherubim) was found with iniquity, violence, and sinned, then cast out of the presence of the creator (Ezekiel 28:11-19, Retrieved from the *King James Version* bible). The manufacturer created another product (Adam) in His image (or likeness) with components (or features) including the diaphragm, lungs, and larynx[14] with the ability to create melody. Music is the product expressing the manufacturer's nature through melody in an environment. In addition, music is the product expressing its own nature independent of the manufacturer through melody in an environment. Music is an expression of everything in heaven. In addition, music is an expression of everything under Heaven in seasons of time including:

- time to be born

- time to die

- time to plant

- time to pluck up that which is planted

- time to kill

- time to heal

---

[14] The larynx, commonly called the voice box, is an organ in the top of the neck of tetrapods involved in breathing, producing sound, and protecting the trachea against food aspiration. The larynx houses the vocal cords, and manipulates pitch and volume, which is essential for phonetics.

Discovering the Purpose of You, the Product

- time to break down
- time to build up
- time to edify or instruct
- time to encourage or inspire
- time to weep
- time to laugh
- time to mourn,
- time to dance
- time to cast away stones
- time to gather stones together
- time to embrace
- time to refrain from embracing
- time to gain
- time to lose
- time to keep
- time to cast away
- time to be happy or joyful
- time to rend or be sad
- time to sew
- time to keep silence

The Manufacturer's Manual

- time to speak
- time to love
- time to hate
- time of war
- time of peace
- time to eat

Music can play an important part in meditation. Music can help to calm and strengthen the spirit of man. It is important that music used in meditation is used to underscore and echoes the manufacturer's instructions in His manual. Music that carries a contrary message will contradict the effect of the sensible study of the manufacturer's manual. Music holds a distinctive influence to establish its tempo or pattern in your mind. Did you ever have a song affect your sub-conscious to such a point you find yourself automatically or involuntarily singing it? Certain music will engraft itself in your spirit and cause you to grow up (mature), grow out (of negative character deficiencies), and grow into (the creator's or manufacturer's intentions). Satanic, evil, or soulish music is not able to plant or cultivate life in your heart but becomes a wicked force to distract from your life by planting ungodly or evil seeds for your sub-conscious to meditate on. Sometimes, a person's soul is disquieted by the approaching situations, challenges, or difficulties in life. Music supports in silencing the noise and quieting the soul to hear the voice of the creator (or Father) and bring help or remedies.

Discovering the Purpose of You, the Product

Notes and Insights

The Manufacturer's Manual

Chapter 15

Media

The Manufacturer's Manual

A small percentage of US population is involved in media production. Through the presentation(s) of drama and special effects, the media production industry (including books, newspapers, magazines, flyers, billboards, automated telemarketing, movies, television broadcast, radio broadcast, internet articles, and social media post) has a very large impact in our lives, including the way we think and act. Media indirectly influences commerce, culture, and politics. For example, media is used in the US by the political system and allows the public to see and hear candidates throughout an election process. In addition, media highlights political issues and social problems for a broad or small audience. Politicians participate in mass media for self-promotion purposes, including broadcasting political advertisements, making television interviews and appearances, publishing articles and essays, and exchanging information through social media. The media is a valuable commodity. In the United States, corporations control most of the media. However, in countries such as China and Russia, the national government controls the media, also known as state media.

Where do political attitudes or opinions come from? Is it based on what type of family structure someone is a part of, what gender someone is, and/or what religion if any someone is a part of? These factors play an important role in how the media influences our political and social attitudes. Keep in mind that many political decisions are carried out by political leaders in back rooms. A political decision is any choice dealing with governmental affairs, social structure or climate and/or religious activities. In the United States before the 1970s, political leaders selected political candidates, the popular political issues, and directed the political process. By the 1970s, candidates and officials frequently presented issues and themselves directly to the voters through the use of television. As a result, the voters started

Discovering the Purpose of You, the Product

placing a higher value on the personality and character of candidates and officials. Rather than researching an issue, problem, or topic, the voter trusts that potential elected candidates and officials will make the right decision. The voter's attitude on how to vote, volunteer, and who to contribute money to is shaped by the media's coverage. In addition to politics, media assists in forming opinions about race, gender, sex, religion, money, marriage, travel, transportation, education, food, and clothes purchased.

The watching of programs or listening to programs through media is not a substitute for the ongoing care of a pastor and assembling with believers to facilitate growth. The media can be used as a supplement to help reinforce what is being consumed through the ears and eyes of those under the care of pastors, shepherds, bishops and/or elders during the shepherd's work. A dietary supplement is a manufactured product intended to supplement the diet when taken by mouth as a pill, capsule, tablet, or liquid. A supplement provides the extra nutrients needed and is extracted from natural food sources or artificial sources to increase the quantity of nutrients consumed. With the the ongoing care of a pastor and with active assembly with believers, media can be used to aid (or enhance) the understanding of information, reinforce the creator's intent for His product (mankind), and facilitate maturity in everyone.

The Manufacturer's Manual

Notes and Insights

Chapter 16

Message to the Nations from the Creator (Manufacturer)

The Manufacturer's Manual

Just like every boy becomes a man, and every girl becomes a woman, every product becomes great when its purpose is fulfilled. The product's purpose is set before it is created. The Bible is the Manufacturer's Manual to Humanity operating within prescribed measurements, boundaries, and/or limits to fulfill the purpose, safeguard the product, and to have an intimate (close and friendly) relationship with the product. Much of human history is composed of the product (mankind) attempting to operate independently of the creator. The goal of the creator is an intimate (close, warm, friendly) relationship (or connection) as Father with His product. Reading the Manufacturer's Manual will assist the product (mankind) in navigating through its various operations throughout the product's lifespan and create an intimate relationship with the manufacturer. When the product is rightly positioned, the product is rightly positioned for:

- Physical needs like food, water, clothing, housing, transportation, and health to be met,

- Social and relationship needs like friendship and companionship,

- Emotional needs like peace, joy, and deliverance from envy, jealousy, and worry,

- Psychological needs like avoidance of becoming stressed out and/or burned out,

- Security needs like protection,

- Self-significance and self-worth,

- Purpose, assignment, and destiny.

Discovering the Purpose of You, the Product

Submission of the product in right positioning (or right attitude) to the manufacturer keeps the product operating correctly. Submission to the manufacturer involves levels of communication and communion during the lifetime of the product (identified in figures below).

Level I

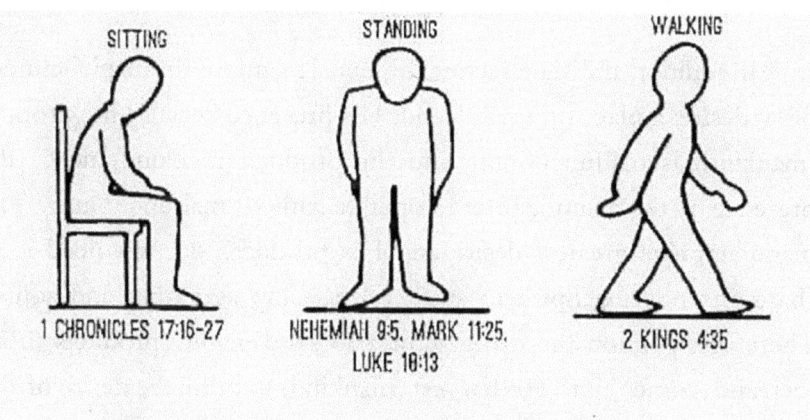

Level II

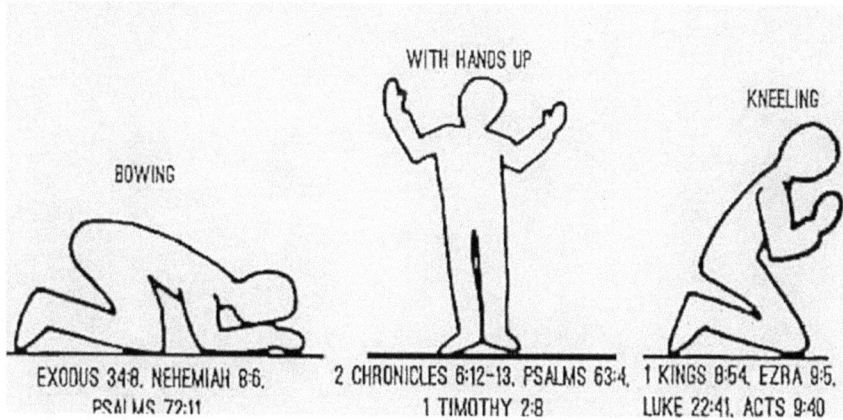

The Manufacturer's Manual

Level III

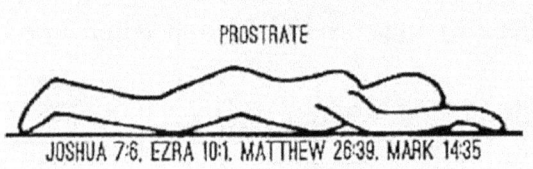

In addition, the Manufacturer's Manual mentions the manufacturer's basic desire: a place on earth to put His presence because the product (mankind) is malfunctioning and the product (mankind) needs the presence of the manufacturer to operate without malfunctioning. The manufacturer's greatest desire and His product's deepest need is to share an enduring Spirit to spirit relationship as Father and son(s). Therefore, petition the manufacturer to send mature products (both men and women) into His harvest (mankind) to fulfill the desire of the manufacturer.

Discovering the Purpose of You, the Product

Notes and Insights

The Manufacturer's Manual

About the Author

The Manufacturer's Manual

Allen Wilson is originally from New York City. He was born to Calvin J. Smith (deceased) originally from Washington, North Carolina, and Willie D. Wilson originally from Albany, Georgia. Allen Wilson served the United States of America in the US Air Force for 22 years. He continues to serve as an ambassador (diplomat, envoy, and emissary) in the Kingdom of God (also known as (aka) Ambassador Scott). A king has a crown. The crown of a king is his wife. He has been married to his crown, Marsha A., for 30 years. He and his wife have three sons Jorell, Jared, and Jeremiah.

References

Batmanghelidj, F MD (1997), *Your Body's Many Cries for Water,* Global Health Solutions, Inc, Falls Church, VA

Cooper, Calottta (2012), *The Complete Beginner's Guide to Raising Small Animals,* Atlantic Publishing Group, Ocala, FL

Damazio, Frank (1988), *The Making of a Leader,* City Bible Publishing, Portland, OR

Day, Lorraine MD (1998), *Diseases Don't Just Happen,* Rockford Press, Thousand Palms, CA

Fletcher, Kingsley (2000), *The Power of Covenant,* Regal Books, Ventura, CA

Keenan, Edward (1973), The Art of the Possible, An Everyday Guide to Politics, Owlkids Books Inc, Berkely, CA

Jordan, Bernard (1989), *Mentoring-The Missing Link,* Zoe Ministries, Brooklyn, NY

The Manufacturer's Manual

Jordan, Bernard (1991), *Meditation A Key to New Horizons in God*, Zoe Ministries, Brooklyn, NY

Lee, George, D III (1994), *Godly Wisdom in Building the Local Church*, Church Builders Ministries

Mendez-Ferrell, Ana August (2005), *The Spirit of Man*, Voice of the Light Ministries, Ponte Vedra, FL

Munroe, Myles (2007), *Applying the Kingdom*, Destiny Image Publishers, Inc Shippensburg, PA

Prince, Derek (1971), *Five Main Ministries CDMM1*, Derek Prince Ministries International, Charlotte, NC

New Analytical Bible (1973), *King James Version*, World Bible Publishers, Iowa Falls, IA

CIA World Factbook - The best country factbook, http://www.ciaworldfactbook.us/index.html

Official Baseball Rules 2018 Edition (2018) ISBN 978-0-9961140-6-6, http://mlb.mlb.com/mlb/official_info/official_rules/official_rules.jsp

What is Asthma, https://www.webmd.com/asthma/guide/what-is-asthma#1

Appendix

Wisdom Keys

Wisdom is always crying in the streets.

A man that does not rule over his own spirit is like a city that is broken down and without walls.

Woe to the land, when the slave (or child) becomes king without a tutor.

His word is like medicine to all your flesh.

His word is health to all your flesh.

The leaves of trees are for healing for the nations.

Water is the lubricant of the physical body.

We must be understood from the inside out, not from the outside in since we are spiritual beings first and foremost.

The Manufacturer's Manual

Everything rises and falls on leadership.

When the blind leads the blind, everyone falls into the pit.

Our man-made laws can't change the nature of a product.

Don't judge the Creator (or yourself) by your last experience because your last experience was based on your level of experience and your level of understanding at that time.